D1528859

REMEMBERING
THUNDER

REMEMBERING THUNDER

POEMS BY

ANDREW GLAZE

NEWSOUTH BOOKS

Montgomery

NewSouth Books
P.O. Box 1588
Montgomery, AL 36102

Library of Congress Cataloging-in-Publication Data

ISBN 1-58838-077-7

Design by Randall Williams
Printed in the United States of America

ACKNOWLEDGMENTS

Some of the poems in this volume have appeared in the following publications:
"Notes On a Gumwrapper" and "If That Mocking Bird Don't Sing," *Birming-
ham Poetry Review*; "Prometheus Who," "Please Take The Joy of It," and "Most
You," *New York Quarterly*; "Thoreau Again," "Yeats and Berryman Have Tea,"
"Bliss," and "Life of Luck," *Negative Capability*; "Ghostwriter" and "Ballad of
Being Gone," *Home Planet News*; "Angels" and "Being Elsewhere," *Rattapallax*;
"A Little Han Horse," *Open Places*; "Miami Storm," "Witch Broom," "A Fall
Gallop," and "Night," *Pivot*; "Horace," *South Florida Classics*; "Sun" and "Day,"
Sarasota Review; "Ballad Of Being Gone" and "Ghostwriter," *Home Planet
News*; "Blue Barouche" and "Remembering Thunder," *Sulphur River*; and
"Here We Come," *Earthwise*.

TO

MARTIN MITCHELL

AND

WILLIAM PACKARD,

WITH BLESSINGS AND THANKS

.

Contents

Four—It Soars Like Hydrogen

Five—Shadows, Even Shadows Dance

ONE

Brains with Wings

PROMETHEUS WHO?

"Man—in apprehension how like a God—"
                                        SHAKESPEARE

How vast it all is! (this mighty rain-slick range)
on which we're spreadeagled, like an eagle dinner,
vaguely lumped together,
only cobwebs tamped with cow-spittle, butt-faced.

We ask and ask, why laid on us the world's madnesses—?
Its chaos rifts in the wild cockpit
of the muddy, bloody plain below.
What can we do to make it right? Christ woe!

Neither Gods nor men, I'm told,—we're Heroes.
But what's a Hero? Who made us so?
Brains with wings, we're born
part of the poison-baited problem,
caught between changes, feigning contrition
for what we don't understand,
and blamed for a vast extremity which only groans.

The Great Oz keeps roaring in our ears,
settle things! Make them right!
(Settle *what* things?)
We?—Who can't even keep our fingernails fastidious!
They unwrap on our birthday horrid exploding things.
Telling us give! Who've nothing to give!

And nobody tells us why! Just that we *ought!*
We listen to eagle pinions,
angry flutterings, the clacking of hungry beaks,
an itch which we can't scratch, shackled to a rock face,
growling with pain.

Only once in a while, does something speak
through the whirligig of hungry birds,
and we scream "What's our punishment for?"
—Answered from above, with a furious growl—,
"for giving them fire!,—"

Yes! Yes! We were mad! Giving fire to those creatures
not one of whom thanks us!
Who only leap about stupidly, flaming,
apprehending nothing,
and haven't the least gift for what we gave.

PLEASE TAKE THE JOY OF IT

(A translation from Osip Mandelstam)

Please take the joy of it, here from my hand,
this little bit of sunshine, this little bit of honey.
They beg me to do it, these bees of Persephone.

Who can cut the moorings of an unfastened rowboat,
who can catch the sound of a shadow with fur feet,
who can trap fear? We live in its thicket.

We wait here for nothing, left only with kisses,
which fall away lost, wandered from the hive.

Rustling, they weave through the hazy night thicket
in their homeland—there in the wood of Taygetus,
browsing on the wild thyme, clover and mint.

Take it for pure joy, this wildness I give you,
my unassuming dried-out pendant and chain,
of dead bees who've turned their honey into sun.

ADMIRING THE RAIN

Admiring the rain, its scupper-ring and rattle,
haunting the eaves,
sad, full of gentle murmur,
we remember what we thought it used to say
before it had so much of us to trouble with.

We proudly made a sort of peace
with that ancient amulet of earswax
found in tombs, that we called hope.
And though our eyes warned us
the world was just as much a brute splash,

a wounded horse drowning in a pond,
this time, we thought, we'd find a grand new breed
of fierce and smoky sunsets spewing
wonders from the tops of our heads,
making an earth of saffron banks like wings.

We'd corner freedom, somehow,
make it what it said it was,—palaces, sunfish,
secrets, deer paths, pine-woods,
fucking turned to love and prophecy.

But underneath, it blossomed still
like a terrible, crimson rose of fear.
And we miss, and miss ever more,
the rain's gentle lapping,
its old-fashioned sort of hand that once
we were proud to grapple tight as we skipped faring.

Yeats and Berryman Have Tea

How grossly mismatched a pair,
and how curious
this once they should meet,
hailing each other like opposing storms.

Uneasily they sit,
duelling, fencing, behind a pair of thin glib smiles!
The Senator with his
bunched white shirt, the hernia,—sort of—
bowties, the Anglo-Irish pox,
the persona of a horribly bothered old man—
who almost holy, palpably, does "gleam."

The other, pupil and guest,
for whom, alas, the inked page
"only, alone, truly, finally cares!"
His lust and rage run out in all aspects,
thinned to inhuman tinctures.
Today, out of courtesy, he's trying
not to look like a young dog
envying an old man's luck.

So, for a space, they sit, beaming and sipping,
tending the decencies—
each one tucking one hand to the neck
and another to the crotch.
Both are accustomed to waltzing towards rape each night,
attending desperate cases,
and through it all, gloriously singing songs.

Loud enough—almost—
to shut out the tapping upon the window at the back—
where toothless, topless banshees knock,
knuckles flame-red,
hailing these two with whorish shriek
as their own, ancient,
soon-to-awaken kings of fear and despair.

NOTES ON A GUM WRAPPER

"Man is the animal that loves violence."
SUPERMAN'S FINAL SENTIMENT

Trailing behind ten thousand years
at last it had caught us. (shriek!)—
That we'd pretend was no worse than fleabite,
scurf, or plaquey teeth.
Some way, couldn't it be outgrown—?
or ogled full in the face.

Have Moses and the Popes
all this era only peed through our telephones?
Are all Utopias only Lenin's brutes,
and the monomaniacal monks and parricides
only mobsters much like me?
What about Art?—
looking absurd in its suicide mission for peace?

Once upon a time,—we had it all explained—.
We kept uprooting Hatred and Torture like an iron anvil,
putting The Truth in armor,
and dropping it with a crash on Justice's feet.
Right would wipe out Wrong once more,
with a satisfying screech!

But butting our heads again and again, that way,
seems finally to have caught us up.
We see that humorlessness is the crime.
Therefore we must learn to laugh,
and laughing frantically, we await our turn to be hung,
counting on our fingers
how no-sense-of-humor is crime number one.

Meanwhile, what we used to trust, love,
melts and is clamped in the stocks, by the God of trade,
and friendliness navigates through icebergs of frowns,
finding it harder all the time, than it used to be,
to wind up the slack—
to beat the gust and the decompression—
to clean the false teeth clacking at the brink?

Forgetting,—blessed, dear, forgetting, that's the ticket,
It will save us as it always has!
Forgetting, loyal friend that every morning
wakens us to luck and leaving go!
With its help, next week
we'll get the star vaults cranking up again
brimming with tumultuous fires!

Silver lines, up-ended, once again will spring
across the sweat-brimmed, grease-paint sky,
cheerfully working at the task of acting God!
Engrossed. In detail. Straining to put him in a good mood!
Acting his merciful smile!

A Little Han Horse

With his tail in a rainbow curve,
his mouth ruffling the air like a golden flute,
his hooves glittering in rapture,
—with cocked ears, he's off—
to what improbable sapphire mountain?
Above the thick reek below of rage and grief,
fire-blasted cities, starving children, skewed old men
proffering grey worn-out eyes
and great bellies, he skims.

But where he goes, also,
is afflicted with wild armies,
furious combustion and loss.
So, he flies as part of it,
through, between, beneath,
hooves flickering sparks, nostrils flaring,
his heart knows it all.
He skips a little dance of joy.

BLUE BAROUCHE

We ride the sling
that casts us spectrally about the sun,
making up misdirections as we fly,
left wing perilous,
right wing down the slope
with stars for nightcap,
scuffing dust for shoes.

But it's never perilous enough for us,
we keep up-raising the bids,
squabbling like infamous biddies and stumble-bums,
trashing the careful, clever direction signs
that make our home home.

If anyone's watching,
what will they make of the bet on ourselves
we're so discounted to?
Perhaps sometime, they'll have to patch it up once more—
our beautiful, battered, blue barouche—
that we spoil,—
and let it spin away
through the firmament on the track
of another less senseless, less ferocious,
not quite so greedy, crew.

SPELIOS

Sure, the textbooks babble.
Things about "Orpheus," and picturesque
lies about nymphs, snakebite, hypnotic singers.
One day a fearsome signal klaxoned "come!"
and something in him was afraid to know
where to.
You reach it by straggling down a path
dark, sloppy, and without aim,
to the gates of Hell.
His way of getting there was from middle Tennessee.
Orpheus slid below from Aornum in Thesprotia.
The gates are shaded with gloomy cedars,
shadowy in frazzled sunlight.

To enter such a place, a cave,
you lie upon your back like being born,
and push against the rock of the strangulated roof
feeling your way below and endlessly down.

He feared it more than death,
such a trap in such a closed place,
but his soul would take no argument.
Orpheus had a lyre for talisman—he had dry lips.
Yet he slid through their gate,
ready to stare in the chops of the king of hell.
Hero to no one but himself, he brought it off.

It's taken him nearly fifty years
to wrestle his soul
out of the power of that dread lord,
to lead it up to earth. To learn that
warned not to look back, you *must* look back.
Without loss, there's nothing *chthonic*.
It's the ugly price you pay for wisdom,
yesterday, tonight, or when Hell sends its bill.

ON BEING ELSEWHERE

Something in me climbed to Heaven's gate—
once—and spoke to the lark.
(It squawked),
a something which heard the dizzy tocsin
of *Die Tochter von Elysium*—
whose dreams somehow came tumbling out of it,
threw themselves in a narrow street
and marched away—clenched like a fist or a heart.

But mostly I have struck with the world
some kind of bungle-headed bargain.
I don't march any more,
I live by a sort of letter box at the porch of things
where every day, notes arrive—one or two.

Where from? What am I being reminded of?
—Why?
And how does each one, as I open it,
release like a bird, fly like a bolt,
leave to my eyes only a snatched glimpse
of lost mountains and burnt ruinous skies?

Fusileer

Somebody taught me—
useless to be a soldier of faith,
who fights for any right, except most everything is wrong.
But coming from a believing crew,
although I strove my best to trust in nothing,
my yes to all that no was a terrible fraud.

Underneath I guarded an equal hope.
If I worked with a furious heart, I thought,
I might do something about a world of money
selling to nothing its blood-soaked line of business grit.
So I kept peddling the fraud to myself
like mottos for the grail
till beaten down every night
nothing was left I could possibly want to prevail.

But anyway, every morning
I wake up like a fusileer,
tie a rag to a stick, and fiercely hoist it high.
Even before I get it to the street,
my heart starts to jig like a monkey on a lead,
marching to fight for a blessed nothing,
with shining eyes and a song.

JUDAS TREE

That awful need of every one of us to suffer—
I've been there a hundred times,
preening like a scrag-top pea-fowl,

—guilty because the mothers of Tigre
scrub in the dirt for spilled grain—
because a stork stabs waterbirds—
because with time-off for slogans
the Chinese wave pointless placards
in front of their masters' guns.

It's because I'm a creature of words,
and though words are nothing but scapegoats,
(we cringe at their brutish thrash).
As Voltaire said,
they cannot change the element,
but we must continue to try.
Daddy said, trust nothing.
That he was right, there is no doubt.
If you can learn to elude the world correctly,
you may survive it at its most atrocious playing out.

But sometimes you must let the dangerous passion
hammer and unbolt your eyes
or hate yourself like a Judas tree.
If you don't risk death, once in a while, for life,
why grieve or love, or take up this minstrelsy?

Thought Wolf

The mind's a wolf
with a hungry belly
that ranges the edges
of the blustery night
through the turbulent cold
shopping the burrows of hares.

With an instant snap
in some icy thicket
it kills and bolts, turns and coils,
rests its face on its tail,
and with a grim grin—
turns within.

Two

Ghosts

Remembering Thunder

Daddy, waving his malacca stick,
taps the fieldstone scarp of the porch.
Over the stormy valley beneath—
and whacking their bows in response—, the cloud armies
jam and collide like a violent opera afternoon
in the rough, crowded spaces
between the ridges of mountain barricades.

"Here, now, arrive the slow squadrons,"
he says with a fierce hiss.
"The elephants are galumphing in
to kneel before the grandees of the durbar.
And here, with a howl from above,
come the Grand Gods, shrieking
apocalypse at the opera."

Next, the rain whacks down
with a splash and a sweeping,
tumbling in mats a clangorous downpour
sheeting and spinning, tieing knots
like ropes about the trees.
The plate-glass water stretches,
rinses between boughs,
the stubborn yews writhe and thump.

"Comes thunder!," shouts Daddy, banging his stick,
like a mad conductor.

"He's a bouncer, with a waist
like a snake in high boots.
See the silver straps?
The way he rolls his shoulders
selling us doom?
Oh, we'll never believe it.
We think underneath he's only a drunk
stopping to piss in the backstage john.
Or maybe a trampy actor, playing Gorky!
Forgive him! Forgive him, for once!
Because he's doing it
not a minute about any money,
but only for the fun!"

SAM, YOU HEAR ME CALLIN'?

Only another old man dying alone,
playing with dregs among the mustache locks,
trapped in the bed wrinkles.
But in some way, Sam's not here, anyway you look.
He's cast off in the raft,
is rapiding off down the river by burning wreckage
booming with ecstasy through the chutes.

Gone with Huck, Jim,
Bilgewater and the Dolphin, floating,
pulling up out of lightning on castaway islands,
beset with rattlers, he's lost
in the burnt ends of steamboat nights—
disappeared in the search which never finds itself.

He's learnt to love that creature, wild,
lover of blood,
not quite bright as a stump—which is us.
But don't dast stop laughing,
else it will turn into rage.

He's gone down that unconsidering river,
seeking perfidy's bandito strand,
hauling it out of the water, spinning it into yarn.
He's tossed one end of the line in the water,
waits with amusement what will take the lure
and make a run with the hook and line today.

Ghostwriter

In memory of Norman Rosten, 1914-1995

It's been only five days now, but reliable
as Mozart, he's already following me around
like a clumsy phantom of winds, reeds,
flies and brown bears. Doppelganger
with the sardonic smile, he took such long pains
to construct himself,—a sort of small-sized, shaggy
aircraft-carrier, emitting flights—,
now he can laugh, hide behind doors,
make great fun of going where he's already gone.
What they call Death is ordinary,
respectable and rude. He doesn't fit.
How can he be giving me prods
and showers of hilarious meaningless threats?
He makes a terrible spook, an incompetent vampire
who's donated all his blood to poems.

Yet no mistaking who's slamming the doors,
creaking on the stairs, fluttering in the glass
with the orange juice. Each wandering electricity
is followed by the smell of its own ozone.
You may throw iron filings in the air as you will,
he's free of exact diagrams. And honored
as I am to be haunted so, I remember there are,
how shall I say,—ever so many others
he'll want to frequent, to honor with his wraithly
touch, that it's pure luck—pure luck!
every one of us—to be dogged by the spirit
of such a generous poltergeist, whatever
side of the door the gift is coming from,
whether going out or coming in.

The Ballad of Being Gone

Where's the old brown Victor AM box
I hurried to on Sunday nights
with half a sandwich of what there was for dinner
and half a sandwich of peanut butter.
Going to visit myself again, and in that place,
that's lately gathered and gone?
Jack Benny's scratching at his violin for Love In Bloom,
and Eddie Cantor singing a sad song
called Making Whoopee.
Ethel Waters piling up clouds of Stormy Weather—alas—
as lost as a puff of wind in the grass.

And, Daddy, chewing his pipe in the northwest chair,
reading a while till his eyes close and he's gone,
and Mama, who's played a Brahms Waltz on the baby grand,
and now, wringing her arthritic hands, takes a nap on the blue
        settee.
Then the lawn in the side yard, its badminton net
where even Woody could never get Sis to play,
and the primal fig tree by the back porch,
where is it dropping its sexual fruit with the red heart?
And the glorious night of the Night Blooming Cereus,
blooming so rarely that people come to see.
Where's that gone?

And that midnight ringing of the phone,
and Saddy advising sulfurous remedies,
wet and hot, to soothe the dolors of the skin,
and where's the shiny near-black mahogany table
near which Emily Dickinson
first made a vast hole in the air and drew me through
and shut the wind behind us?
And where's that brave stony porch against storms,
and the porte cochere, and my lonely sand-pile,
where's what I was,
and where are all our giant, midnight-dark firs?
And our beautiful house of green.

And where's the mountainous lawn and the spiral drive,
and daddy hurrying down deadly, that last hateful night,
falling to headlong ruin by anger destroyed,
the harsh forty-five thrown down on the seat beside him,,
all ready to kill the girl who dared hoodwink him,
and bringing wreckage, the end of all that we knew
of our house and our city and being young,
—gone without remedy, who knows where,—alas—
as lost as a puff of wind in the grass.

MOCKER

That Hope is a catch in the trap of feathers.
a forgetful bird keeps reminding us of,
wandering glorious song to song
beneath a stinging moon.
Then an owl goes past
fluttering with a "chunk."

But until what can't be explained, or so much as heard,
quivers past, making the skin jump,
it's but an amalgam of life, death and failure
trembling in your pulse.

Is it about to arrive, or about to make you wait?
What wants it to have a name?
The answer unintelligibly rummages through the shadows,
losing itself in midnight.

It hides from you where you
wanted to be, once
and what you are now,

and is forever reaching out ahead
stealing away into some remoter kind of darkness
where only the music of silence
makes a guess at what we are to be.

NOTHING

Brainless and dim, it once in a while comes after me.
It slurps along its jowls and yaps like a frisking brute.
It says I'm a puppet, and while jerking my strings,
falls on me like *merde*.
I pretend not to notice, say I won't concede
or bow to aught except what owns my mind.

Still, when it lifts my right, I flop and fly.
When it drops my left, I fall.
No matter how much I battle to clobber it,
already I'm too late, for it has smitten me.
I study to master the craft to make it fail,
the flagrant blister rides inside my hat!

But though it hates me, though it fiercely snarls,
I own a secret passage it can't penetrate.
I hold a secret flaunt it fails to go.
I'm ever somewhere else above it,
even as it grabs my feet.
I'm fanged like a wolf,
but proofed against a fang.
I sing, oh, sing!—the secret music that's my fate!

One Day Summer

What he remembered of Holyhead and Anglesay—.
Was the up as much as down about the street
curled on the headland; the mole that went to sea
ambitiously as though let loose in flight
by some rash traveler off for Enniscorthy,
Shop glasses shining like fish's eyes new tinned
through the glut of the dingy roads—the skies in sheets,
grey blankets, pillows, the rumpled bed of wind.

And one bright day on the mole he walked and watched
two stranded ships in the harbor beached like staves,
two stove-in "Victories" all their ruined wealth
five diving sailors striking seas that blotched,
curdled, and humped. The air drummed with their health.
And he climbed upon the seawall to read the sky.
Too late, he saw his neighbors' eyes like slaves
that bowed, served, and kept their powder dry.

It was a clergyman, who endured the sun
as though such a thing were a burdensome duty.
In a funeral working suit all ash and dust,
like penance for the world, and an ivory ring
for a collar, and lips more fearful of good than frightened
by the lewd. That air of seeking a test—
"—God doesn't have much of this to spare,"
approving the weather, "Until we deserve it next."

So, trapped into talk—the ships in the bay, the weather—
the war—they teetered perilously about that piety
like two old maids ignoring dung they scuttle by all day.
He was asked to tea, and ugh! What a conscience-stricken rite!
His egg, an eye, complacent of his greed. His cake
a half loaf playing martyr for the precious whole.
He hated being made to feel like a rake
in ruins from the wars his pleasures waged,

robbing virtue's body to feed the soul!
Still, he escaped, and found the wind and the harbor
had kept up their sunlit humors and the morning's
drummer still pelted him with fife tunes as he fled.
How is one to answer the assaults of virtue?
If a one day summer is not much warmth, at least,
it's better to scatter a handful of coins for retribution,
and set them to glittering polkas down the street.

Ariel

Dropping his joshes and banters
upon us,
he flutters down the midnight of our system.

How we hate his topsy-turvy wings!
We can't imagine
whether he's got them shut or parceled out,
or when they will open, coruscate and fly.

Wearing the crooked spectacles of the quotidian,
we hail him like an old-fangled businessman
trying to peddle the shimmering and become the cash.

We swat and swat at his fly-dom,
but somebody's got to dance
for the dangerous beauty of the earth,

and we can't however wealthy, buy him out,
so we pin him up like a frog for study,
snip off his wings.

"Hooray," we shout from the chapel of common sense,
"good riddance from this placid boulevard,
pandemonium's cut off and up the spout."

But, come the night, there's always some
unexpected creature
hobbles out and tests the air on clumsy wings,
secretly escaping down shinbone-alley
to deeper in doubt.

If That Mockingbird Don't Sing

Near sunset, one of them flutters
and comes to rest on the dead gleaming
brass antennae tree
up at the peak of Mary's house.
From there it overturns upon our head
a breathtaking babble of song
like, after rain, silver cataracts.

Someone's announcing the month!
But his company soon will be setting up shop,
fluttering through the sticky mangos,
practising on fences, tressilating the tops
of the streetwise mahoganies,
whistling and fluting, dredging up hour-long strains
from the same antique chapbook
out of which my mother used to' practise
songs taught by her mother a hundred years past.
But the mocker's mysterious joyous music
is an intricate score
from nothing but empires of worms and bugs and millipedes.

Falling in with a mate,
they'll begin to pick on the dogs,
the cats, the passing people,
that way letting us know they are building
another generation of treetop organ grinders.

Next year, as I do every year,
when they bring in the Spring with their silvery battery,
I'll listen again to find what greeting it is
they are trying to pass from Mama to me,
from me to her,
and which direction she has strayed off to,
entranced,
lost in that unlikely never-land
of perfect, effortless song.

Most You

You're an old graveyard of dead pangs,
like goat bones, which stood off once and ramped
together, knocking heads, "bock!" and now
can only groan away and creak and bleach and hide.

Somewhere beneath, aren't you as much fire,
as much uncontrollable blood,
as many lashings of desperate remedies,
as ever you were given?

When they try to make you
play the wise old cipher, must you let them have their way?
Between moonlight and dawn,
on top of a hill you know

the queen awaits in her brake of green.
So much older than you'd dare, lovely
as rain, she holds out her eternal arms.
Something like a tear courses down her cheeks,

and all night long, lost in the murmurous haze
of what's most you,
you will grow younger as you grow older,
flattening pennies on the track of the moon.

BLISS

It being brave, and the thing to do,
I gave her my soul.
She found the offer interesting,
wore it awhile like a ring.
But having gone so far,
and it getting dull,
I must bare her my throat.
What a wonderful game!
Her blood raced, my blood raced
(you understand—just in the thought).

Having got to be that much of a wag,
I could see the double-dog dares
would go on and multiply like mice.
Which they did. So I had to choose.
I opted—well—for bliss.
There's nothing wrong with that, I guess,
it's one of the gambles you take.
But the dice rolled—and rolled,
and they came out like this.

Three

Stissing's Children

Thoreau Again

Those green-vaulted pine assemblies,
so to speak—those giant acquaintances,
—living among us like strangers,
take, if anything, a far-off view of the day-to-day,

and the least midge, stinging at my awareness,
lives more beside earth, in it,
dependent upon its daily chance, than I.

But even thinking about it is somehow
to risk losing the way.
Responsibility was a thing we took
—that it never asked.

Even thrashing thoughtlessly
about this blackberry thicket
you'll never suspect there's a bear,
until it rises, nose quaking and steaming.

Perhaps because searching's the gift,
and nothing's like life—but life. What, of all this,
do the pines report?—As much or little
as you wish, but they turn—and keep turning.

You—Archibald Macleish

That day up the hill with Joseph Lordeman, Claverack way,
what it was began to show itself un-resting,
folding and unfolding, the hilltops rolling in all directions,
becoming another morning and—another,
one hundred years, two hundred years ago,
the slow-jointed oxen pairs steaming breathily up
along the hazel-edged passage between the ponds
on early mornings, coming to plough the high fields.

And how
before the cattle and their long rhythmic draft,
the Hurons and their brethren
padding along the ridges after the deer,
slaves like each of us no less
to what keeps witlessly spending.

And how even straddling the globe—
life and death, pain, waves of appetite—
it keeps gobbling the edges with the same tireless motion
used and re-used without our knowing
how it can happen to move, even shut away
and lying still in the cupboards of understanding.

And even with nobody knowing why
and at whose choice it speeds, how it rises
tumultuous and early, then comes to fiercely crest
and fiercely shine, then tumbles over and over
out of the sky all at once
extinguished daily into the boiling broth of tomorrow.

SUN

Flaming golden
in the iron-deep night,
it sings and spins,
wayfares toward morning
through gray sails,
banked curtains,
thoroughfares of cloud.

Reaching our window,
it proffers arm, day, word,
raises itself like a sash,
and then, lost member
of our household
with a returning gift,
clambers unassumingly through.

DAY

All day the orchards
keep raining lakes on the deer,
and the grazing mountains chew
raw cuddy mouthfuls of lush sun,
crammed with surprises like trickling cattle.
The skies rinse over porcelain blue,
and something is making things move,
but from hiding.
You are only able to clutch with your hand
at the fringe of its shawl,
yet how artfully everything living
rolls over stealthily to dusk,
and black and dun, the flanks of the hills
swarm with secret cliffs,
and Phaeton turns to a falling star,
you can smell the burning.
Then, at the top of the hill
he shucks his fiery jacket,
and, quickly as they danced for him to arrive,
the looming mountains
douse the bonfires of victory,
noiselessly roll on their backs, and here comes
        over the Milky Way,
spreading its vast comforter,
sprinkling millions of tacks
that fall like stars
and sleep on the roof of your house.

NIGHT

Night pulls up its cloak and belt,
breathes through its teeth the rain.
Lopside, velvet gait, its heels go tock
down roads swept dark of the moon.

Shadow on shadow, owls in its pockets,
sifting through trees, huffing its wings—
it rests in a crack while the mockingbird plainsongs
through endless drift its ode of change on change
chimed for the ears of foxes.

Sometimes, arms akimbo, it flashes its black boots
weaving and writhing with rumbles of thunder,
thrashing a music through clearing and brake,
erotic as the tremblings of hills.

Or it shakes Black Mountain deep in its roots,
and breathes in life as it sighs out death.
Its name it whispers is whippoorwill wing.
An empire grown secretly great as the chitterings of bats.

COPSES

The arch of frozen night decongeals
to skeins of watery talk.
Stars once hard as pins
pluck at the roof and faintly sing.
Venus is backed up at the moon—
but firm as a bolt,
it stares sullenly—nothing to say.
Still, something's made a difference,
there's a stirring beneath,
the whispered argument begins
in tangled hedge and root,
and already something
has started to clatter the bells off-key,
which faintly, faintly,
join the far off drums of victory
and quiver about
the quarreling copses of March.

Hello—Goodbye

After a life of luck, scrabbling about these streets
where nothing's settled ever but contrary weather
we watch astonished as the globe revolves
on faultless gimbal-pins of prayers.

As though God, with livid whorl and puffing lips,
were blowing on the tubas of storm, and
sun moon and stars crouched
at the foot of some galactic wall.

Would it were more than legerdemain.
On splendid summer afternoons we ache
to snatch one look across the widening chasm of Him
or to cross the dubious footbridge to who knows where.
We want to awake and sleep to epiphanies.

But never mind those lonely paternosters of parley and whine!
They're only foolishness!
Other than a handshake over the widening murk,
weather sliding about its tremulous corner—
and friendship kissing us goodbye as it sails,
there's nothing much waiting for our call.

We begin to ache for departure the moment we become,
and wave to it passing, spitting out the night before.
Wanting is the only taste that lasts.
The world is wishing itself farewell, even as it says hello.
As simply as we do, you and I.

WAKING AND SLEEPING

The sun boils down at the edge of the burning earth,
and the moon, glowering, cold as an ice chunk,
floats up over the life-and-death hungry wood.

Somewhere distant the mockingbird's cantillation
putters across the white gleaming,
trickles from leaf shadow to leaf shadow,
in a serenade to somehow
that skirts the hoot owl's fort, making the skin quicken.

Then, all at once,
it's as though God—stately—had stopped his dancing,
undoing for an instant the owl's rape,
the wolf's rasp, the earth's frenzy.

It's less than a second—
—less than a blink—
but, for that long—humbling our hateful hearts—
and not for any reason we can name—,
it celebrates in the earth's honor
whatever wakens and sleeps.

A Fall Gallop

Today's on a gallop,
barreling through trees by the towpaths,
thundering through tunnels,
battering with sledges at covered bridges,
hallooing past turtle-towns that hunker down
into hiding by the kingdom of way.

Off fieldward,
here's a dozen hay-high blackbirds
whirled up the sky with blood-streaked wings
crashing in the ears of the fact-finding sun.

And now, wind whips off its shirt,
swipes at the ladder-back clouds,
overturns a whole field trespassing west.

The earth is rapt.
Life's upturned like a bucket
and Truth's gone swimming, whirled with the leaves,
shaking beads out of its sprinkled hair.
Nothing has put away till tomorrow
whatever matter-of-fact it wanted to say.

Here We Come

Like a morning's spasm
of butterfly
clapped in sun glitter,
or a wood mouse
bushwacked in the open,
we scurry about our troubles.

Welcoming the bread milled daily
from star-dough like fierce wheat,
we peer through curtains
at things even madder.

Overhead, God speeds his usual
spend-thrift fashion
through trillions of star-fires,
and the farther we stare,
we stare ever more alone
up oceans of nowhere.

Still, here we come anyway,
scattering like seed-thrift
what little we know,
before us in child-steps
as though we'd at last
tracked down manna
in the rubbish
of a sun-wasted speck,
and found there our center.

YIN AND YANG

Lincoln says a great word, Horace Greeley coughs.
Even as babies are proclaimed,
someone elsewhere is opening the graves.
Machetes are the kings of bananas,
oil cabals plot under the sand
where Navajos danced silver into wings,
and over the spotless tree-blue mountain
storm clouds rattle with thunder and whirling dirt.

Villainous, black wind-tree,
bring up your hundred million floods!
They make a hundred billion secret flowers!
See how many dry sticks more will burst into flame
than you can ever learn to put them out!

THEFT

Love, come love me just this once
only for the sake of letting go.
We're in no danger of starting another soul
on the treacherous path.
We only live at the amorous fringes
stealing a moment from youth's consolation,
that sweet payment
for being young and taking the burden,
against the savage weight of the don't-give-a-damn world
with no help and no armor
but danger.

For these new at it, a place to flee to.
For us, balanced on the knife of staying us,
for a little while yet,
it's a stolen ration Aphrodite overlooked
and this is the back door to her temple.
Come, steal the key.
Hand in hand, we'll sneak by the altar
and swipe what she's overlooked.

FOUR

It Soars Like Hydrogen

Moon-Bus

Its bright
silly canoe
sailing down Ninth Avenue
like St. Brendan's barque,
followed, underneath
by the evening star,

then it comes to the bus bridge below
that crosses the end of the street,
like a great brick bow.
Poor silly!
The writ of the port
does not run where it docks,

it has no number, bay or route.
is penniless,
no one can count its change.
But we've such a need for it.
Oh, lover's last transport!

LEARN TO WANT

"Even with that seal through your ear,
you are not the average run of pig,"
they cheer.

"You're the circus!" they tell you. "So, Perform!"
"—Me, oink?"—you philosophise—
"Why should I want to, for this?
—who needs the duties or the pay?"
"Then *learn to want!*"—they reason, cocking the gun.

So, you cycle through life, circling across the stage
two hundred thousand miles, the audience beguiled
fiddling your fiddle, upside down, with tail and hoof,
and on the handlebars, jaws and trotters
bleeding, sore, but thrilled.

When, at last, creation has you wanting what *it* wants,
it placidly explains
that that's how things are justified.

And then, of course, one morning, tippy toe,
waving its handkerchief at you cheerily
it whispers—"look—you're good as dead,
and no more use to us,—so—

there being no lawyer who'll admit he's a swine,
and you not having a contract you can hold us to,
—with a blast of trumpets, you are declared free!—
We'd appreciate your leaving these premises
where you've lived all your days.
in—say
—twenty minutes, else we'll summon the law."

"Go with our blessings, it's been grand,
but shoo!—shoo! pig!—and apocalypse and tea,
but get it through your head
you're a pig, and remain a pig,
however many a grandiose word,
purple choker, and PhD!"

Floating Becomes Ophelia

(A Nashville whine for the 400th anniversary of Hamlet, 2000)

Sometimes I wake up crying,
I'm floating down the stream,
while lily pads and bromeliads
strew flowers in my dream.

Come listen while I'm crying,
my life's too sad to be true.
my love, I find, is out of his mind,
he's run my daddy through.

My tears would fill a dry ravine
'cause I see the signs I fear.
What hurts the most, Hamlet met a ghost
that breathes lies in his ear.

Oh, woe is me, I'm floating
cause the king is bad, to boot.
A terrible thing, that Claudy the King
is a treacherous galoot!

I'll float and cry come double,
while he sends for R. and G.
Who've got in bad with that mizzuble cad
as Hamlet debates to be.

Who wouldn't want to be crying,
they've all drunk a poisoned cup,
and death writes the scorecard with calls from the graveyard
again they've dug Yorick up.

So it's time to be screeching and moaning,
no life preservers for me,
as the gaffers and grips come to cart off the stiffs
I'll float down the stream to the sea.

So you see why I wake up crying,
no relief in sight, oh, gee!
As the gaffers and grips come to cart off the stiffs
I float down the stream to the sea.

The Country Cowboy's Lament Did I Give It to You or Did You Give It to Me?

I met you at the coroner's ball,
already you were pale.
You made me laugh,
with your strength of a half
but I was proud
when you said that you'd come home with me.

We danced at Vegas after three
your face was flushed and gray.
As I put you to bed,
you were good as dead
but sick as a thief
you still said you'd come home with me.

We line-danced for months
all tubes and shots
You sweated when you screamed.
But I was true
and you coughed that you
were proud to still come home with me.

I'll be singing in bars
sometime in a land
as far away as a cow.
Though you've gone to our home
all skin and bone
you live still in my mournful guitar.

Did I give it to you
or did you give it to me?
In this pearly land never mind.
I'll take off my crown
and lay it down
if you will still come home with me.

CENTRAL PARK SOUTH

The sun is moving like an electric yacht
across the smart blue combers of the buildings
splendid in the whitecaps of their rents.
It sails, richly clad, across the square,
about which prince-and-princesses of plumbing
stoop in flight to sleep away the day.
The emerald trees are bred by Tiffany out of Fabergé.

Thou lady up high, I kneel to thee.
To thy pink and chalcedony pants.
Invite me to thy flowery balcony,
feed me, care for me, I promise to write
nothing but rich poems in praise of poverty.
Unless—that's not champagne, that's envy
froths in my neck like foam, lady, fills me up
from the ankle and pops the cork of my chin.
Hell freeze you, donna!
My fist shakes itself. Wilt your plants!
And may all your sons be bankrupt businessmen!

FIVE

Shadows, Even Shadows Dance

GENERATION

I know my generation is to come
by the few who've arrived so far,
eyes damp and lidded,
who get by on lost luggage and wildflowers,
living with one side bound
in the old flesh
flapping like wind-starved sails.

They wait to be thrust into life
untied, unharried and unreduced,
foretold to be fantastic
the way of a two-headed eagle with fangs.

In my sleep I babble about their coming.
It's a double thought
of the warlock edge of the mind,
and whatever window I'm not at,
I sense those impossible brothers and sisters
rushing toward me, hear
their flyway and wing-thrust, as they
hover, shutter their pinions,
and clamber invincibly through.

MIAMI STORM COMING ON

Rain, like exhilaration, slaps its glove on the face,
and down by the dock
plunging hard from the East
run monstrous clouds, thundering over
in shaggy herds like buffalo.
They dig up flying turf plugs with their hooves
in the maddened gray-green tidal water,
their butting heads trail spittle-threads of rain.

Right by me, palmettos strain and flap, shudder
and tear loose,
and up the rebellious sky
darkness comes on,
still bucking and running away, crazy with life,
its nightmares guide the furious beasts
through the perilous fields of froth.

Then the light, struggling in multiple explosions,
fails,
and across the seaway
islands magically rise of a sudden
in multiple shimmerings of low condominium lights.
A vagrant helicopter
thumps and putters circling to the west.

Miracles are a sort of meat grown on desire,
we're made of wilder things than we can admit,
so once in a while, as though by accident,
the glorious beast of the world
for an instant will let us see
how it spins, every hour, without a sign of strain,
endless heavenly wisdom out of trash.

To A Young Man on His 254th Birthday

Wolferl, young friend, what about
all this fal-lal and hoorah?
Oh, you'd love the performances,
no doubt of that!
You wrote somebody once
that on taking a theater seat,
hearing the orchestra begin to tune,
immediately, you were beside yourself.

They've got a thing at Salzburg
involving the house where you were born.
Probably you felt about the place as fiercely
as anyone does about the place they were born.
It's a place.

But we're speaking of serenades—
And three companies recording the same opera
in the same hall, with different people,
in six weeks. Remarkable!
Too bad you won't get any of the royalties.

It is bound to come to someone
before the year's over, to dredge
Vienna's Central Cemetery like a potato farm.
Wanted: medium skull, with small cephalic index,
probably Alpine; prominent nose, tracery upon
the brain pan in C clefs.

A useless labor, certainly, the climate and all.
They'd some to-do, a while ago,
to re-unite the lower Papa Haydn
with his wandering head-piece.
Probably it's just as well you've lost.
Some enthusiastic zealot might bite off your finger,
as some idiot bit off St. Francis Xavier's toe.
Rest your bones.

How? Rest? Well, possibly not.
Certainly they laid you out by force.
That and Papa's religious prejudice about
vaccination. I doubt if you care to rest.
But it's true you sang a bit of the requiem
there at the end. Still, I think it was,
as always with you, the enjoyment of pathos.
Life as the dramatist!
Always the man standing behind the man
standing behind the mask.
You probably thought of death
as postlude-prelude; paying the price,
settling yourself in a cheap seat somewhere
to listen for the tuning of the orchestra.
On hearing it, you'd be
beside yourself at once.

Truth Beneath Truth

Somewhere lost between ghost-hour and subway pallor,
I waken, as I perpetually do,
coming to account to myself for me.

How I was that gentle boy toiling dolefully
to build a small castle out of the earth's sorrow in the sand
because he was taught the world was an ignorant hateful place.

Who never once expected gentle goodness or kind wishes,
and even scratching appearance down to bedrock,
keened for Elysium, never expecting to find it.

And then by luck, along the way, who discovered
how to birth the world
into life out of words, and to reach among them like a clutch
of fingerlings, seething with joy, to make a sort of dance of use.

Now my time too has come to stand homeless as we all must,
along these reedy shores, these egret fluttering shallows,
and watch as the world goes by on its ramping, splashing,
garrulous usual way.

And I'm more or less reconciled to feeling the fool
    and taking the blame,
because the world needs our blame. Because what
    I always wanted
is right. There *are* heroes. There *are* enemies. Foolish or not,

I find I must imitate that fierce bard on myth hill,
    who, head chopped off,
blind, and bleeding, continued to joyfully prophesy.
    Taking him as counselor,
I dance and sing the words I'd sooner be dead than fail to say.

An Unexpected Corner

He comes out of the wood
which is not a wood
in the light of the fiercely
seething moon.
A Harlequin's face
sits upon his face,
Uncertainly he leads by the hand
a lady. She has not entrusted him
with her departure
nor her arrival.

It is unbearably bright, vein by vein.
The creatures peering through the leaves
promise nothing—nothing—nothing—,
why does he adventure on,
cheerfully
through the empty clearing,
beneath such a naked sky?

HORACE

Horace commanded a legion at Phillipi
(like any honest poet, for the wrong side).
Later he joked he'd thrown his shield away,
stealing the posture from Archilochos.

The tricks don't change, only the circumstance.
You navigate the gulfs of ugliness
with the wits intact. It's a game.
Never let them know who you are.

He wasn't too proud to be Augustus's PR man
(the Romans were a tough case),
but as soon as he dared, he picked up his shield again,
and watching from afar, blamed the world on avarice.

The war went on even as now, in the human heart.
and he saw the poet's job
was to hate the hatefulness—

like Walt, to nurse the hurt, and reconcile—.
Like Emily—toughest of all,
to hide in the country with no sign of a shield
and testify to the glory in the soul.

Witch Broom

I ride—at who dares guess what height—
on a witch broom,
flapping in the frost.

It stopped near my head,
shimmered and seethed,
said, "Climb up with me."

I asked advice of my chartered clerk.
"It's only a dragonfly," he advised,
not troubling to look.

Seeing anthems spinning in its wings,
I asked Mr. Audubon. He nodded and shrugged,
"Naught but a lark."

So, not insisting on knowing
what it was I was being offered,
or if it could be believed,

or why it had chosen me,
cheerfully,
up I tripped.

Once it had me, fiercely, it bucked,
and dragged me to creation's rim.
"Get out! Get out!"

Along the way, hopelessly, I heard somebody call.
But it's late—too late—
now getting out, itself,

like Hell, would be a kind of falling.
And at last,
we've come to be sewn together like friends.

It's shown me a sort of dawn rising.
And where am I to find again, on earth,
a way so quicksilver, clandestine and wild,

so heart-stupefying, as this?
To fly and yet not fly.
To sing and yet not sing.

To move every day through myths
that crack like a door
in the wakeful dream of a child.

ANGELS

Through the rain one day
as dolefully I watched, from under the awning
of the gum and candy store,
up past the nearest corner came floating,
—*angels!*—
—they parted like geese with white umbrellas
passing each side the chimney tops.

I leapt to clutch at their trouser cuffs,
but, unconcerned,
they floated up past the tingling streetlights
out of reach, and I missed.

Panicky, I knelt at the pavement's edge
and scrubbed dirt into my hands as much as to say
—I'm not a spirit,—I'm dirt, damn it!
Without this dirtness, I'm not me—.

And everywhere about me, myriad dirt creatures
marched across my hand, sniffed, spat, crapped,
reassured, as though the whole dirt world
were running to my assistance,
and identified itself with me,
in a fierce demonstration of what I swear is so.

But I don't run errands in that block any more.
I'd panic if I saw a flock of them
at their work
—I guess you might call it work—
building impossible cities upstairs,
brick by brick, wall by wall,
out of nothing at all, nothing at all, nothing at all.

Prop Wash

That was not me, aching to fly,
zig-zagging overhead past them all, in my crate of canvas,
stirruping my palomino motor that curvetted in panic,
jumping and spitting green at the fields far below
where cattle rubbed their leather capes
on the snag-wire fences.

But it was me, playing the game at its most myself,
when I climbed up ladders into DC-3s,
and wobbled aloft with creaking pilots
who flew by the raveled seats of their pants, guided only
by the slithers of demon coasters.

Then at last came a time when my wits grew businesswise,
and I teamed up with a world which bought me
to tend its dollary affairs like squadrons
of busy, black, horse-drawn funeral coaches.
And I sounded for years like the dolorous fog-horns
of misty harbors we passed as we clip-clopped away.

But the best wasn't lost, only slipped down a crevice
of some old leather baggage,
and I still hear it whispering, faintly,
the ghost of the prop wash.

Somewhere high, nose set at the limit,
in my most secret moments,
I gasp and I cough at an uttermost ceiling
till my wings tumble over,
and down I come skirring like the bellow of thunder,
firing wild bursts at forever, singing.

About the Author

ANDREW GLAZE was born in Tennessee and raised in Birmingham, Alabama. After graduating with a degree in English from Harvard in 1942, Glaze spent four years in the Air Force and a year in graduate school at Stanford, before returning to Birmingham to work as a reporter during the civil rights movement. His first major book of poetry, *Damned Ugly Children*, published in 1966 (when Glaze was forty-four) was on the Notable List of the American Library Association and was a runner-up for the Pulitzer Prize. He has published eight other books of poetry, all of which, though controversial, have been widely and favorably reviewed. Glaze now lives in Miami, Florida.